Life on the western plains

When we think of American Indians, we usually think of Indians living in tipis and roaming the western Plains on horseback.

But for most of their history, the Indians of the American Plains hunted on foot. The early tribes were small and scattered. They had a hard life, with prairie temperatures that dropped well below zero on windy winter nights and soared in the relentless heat of summer. Since there were few trees to break the wind or give protection and little wood to build with, the early Indians had no natural shelters. They built their houses from the skins of the animals they hunted or from the soil under their feet.

Some tribes that farmed lived most of the year in villages of earthlodges, but used tipis on hunting trips. Dogs were used to carry the small tipis,

belongings and even little children. Then, about 400 years ago, Spanish explorers brought horses to North America from Europe. The Indians welcomed the horse as a miracle and soon were among the best horsemen in the world. Many Indians stopped farming and returned to roaming the prairie, living a nomadic life. The buffalo became easy to hunt from horseback and it provided food, clothing and shelter.

When Europeans began to move westward two hundred years ago, they found the prairies occupied by powerful and organized Indian tribes. But not for long. The white man brought with him war, alcohol and diseases like smallpox. By 1900, most Indians who were still alive were on reservations.

The homes of the Plains Indians – the tipi and the earthlodge – show a love and respect for the earth. The circle that forms the main shape of both shelters is a symbol of the earth. The four sides of the tipi stood for the sun, moon, earth and sky. The earthlodge's domed roof was a symbol of the way the sky covers the world. Inside, every family member had a special place, just as each person had a special role on earth.

dog travois

3

4

Windswept and empty, the Great Plains spread west to the Rocky Mountains

**Native dwellings:
Plains Indians**

Bonnie Shemie

Houses of hide
and earth

Tundra Books

Published in Canada by Tundra Books, Montreal, Quebec H3Z 2N2

Published in the United States by Tundra Books of Northern New York, Plattsburgh, N.Y. 12901

Distributed in the United Kingdom by Ragged Bears Ltd., Andover, Hampshire SP11 9HX

Library of Congress Catalog Number: 91-65369

Canadian Cataloging in Publication Data

Shemie, Bonnie, 1949-
    Houses of hide and earth

ISBN 0-88776-269-7 hardcover 5 4 3
ISBN 0-88776-307-3 softcover 5 4 3 2

(Issued also in French under title: *Maisons de peaux et de terre*.
ISBN 0-88776-271-9)

1. Indians of North America – Great Plains – Dwellings – Juvenile Literature.
I. Title.

E78.G73S515 1991   j392.36'008997   C91-090245-3

Design by Rolf Harder & Associates, Montreal

Printed in Hong Kong by the South China Printing Co. (1988) Ltd.

Also by Bonnie Shemie:

Houses of snow, skin and bones: Native dwellings of the Far North
Houses of bark: Native dwellings of the woodland Indians
Houses of wood: Native dwellings of the Northwest Coast
Mounds of earth and shell: Native dwellings of the Southeast
Houses of adobe: Native dwellings of the Southwest

Acknowledgments:
The author/illustrator would like to thank Dr. J. Daniel Rogers, Associate Curator of Anthropology at the National Museum of Natural History, Smithsonian Institution, Washington, D.C., and Dr. Ted Brasser, Dunrobin, Ontario, for their comments, suggestions, and advice. She also wishes to acknowledge the help of Maggie Blackkettle of the Saskatoon Indian Cultural Centre, Saskatoon, Saskatchewan; Harvey Markowitz at the D'arcy McNickle Center of the History of the American Indian, Newberry Library, Chicago; and Dr. Katherine Pettipas, Curator of Historic and Contemporary Native Studies, Manitoba Museum of Man and Nature, Winnipeg. She would also like to thank the people of the Crazy Horse Memorial, Crazy Horse, South Dakota; the Glenbow Museum, Calgary; the Field Museum of Natural History, Chicago; the Notman Photo Archives, McCord Museum, McGill University, Montreal; the Public Archives, Ottawa; and the Wheelwright Museum, Santa Fe, New Mexico, for their cooperation. She would especially like to thank her brother, Bill Brenner, for his encouragement and advice in writing this book.

Bibliography:
Bodmer, Karl, *Karl Bodmer's America*, Lincoln: University of Nebraska Press, 1984.
Frazier, Lee, "A Reporter at Large; Great Plains," *The New Yorker*, Feb.-Mar. 1989.
Grinnell, George, *Blackfoot Lodge Tales: The Story of a Prairie People*, New York: C. Scribner's Sons, 1892.
Howard, James, *The Canadian Sioux*, Lincoln: University of Nebraska Press, 1984.
Jenness, Diamond, *The Indians of Canada*, 7th edition, Toronto: University of Toronto Press, 1977.
Koerte, Arnold, *Toward the Design of Shelter Forms in the North*, Winnipeg: University of Manitoba Press, 1974.
Laubin, Reginald and Gladys, *The Indian Tipi, Its History, Construction, and Use*, Norman: University of Oklahoma Press, 1957.
Mandelbaum, David G., *The Plains Cree*, Regina: University of Regina, 1979.
McClintock, Walter, "Painted Tipis and Picture-Writing of the Blackfoot Indians," and "The Blackfoot Tipi," Los Angeles: Southwest Museum Leaflets, Southwest Museum, from *The Old North Trail or Life, Legends and Religion of the Blackfeet Indians*, London: MacMillan, 1910.
McCracken, Harold, *George Catlin and the Old Frontier*, New York: Bonanza Books, 1959.
Morgan, Lewis Henry, *Houses and House-Life of the American Aborigines*, Chicago: University of Chicago Press, 1965.
Nabakov, Peter and Easton, Robert, *Native American Structures*, New York: Oxford University Press, 1989.
Neihardt, John G., *Black Elk Speaks: Being the Life Story of a Holy Man of the Oglala Sioux*, as told to John G. Neihardt (Flaming Rainbow), New York: William Morrow, 1932.

only in the river valleys and foothills did trees provide wood and shelter.

The tipi

The tipi cover was made out of buffalo skin, called hide. When a tipi was taken down, it was folded and put on top of the poles. These poles were attached to the sides of a dog, who pulled them with the back ends dragging on the ground. Later, horses carried tipis the same way and the tipis became bigger and heavier.

The tipi, large or small, was very comfortable; soft fur and nice smelling brush kept it fresh inside. As the cover of the buffalo hide got older, it let more and more light through, and at night, with a cooking fire inside, the tipi looked like a glowing cone.

The tipis belonged to the women. They had the job of putting them up and taking them down, and they could do it very quickly. A camp of families that included the very young and very old and all their belongings could be ready for travel in a few minutes.

Tipis were built with wood poles, stakes and pins, a hide cover and ropes. A basic frame of three or four long, straight poles of pine or red cedar was tied together near the top and set upright. All the other poles except one were leaned on these to form a cone. The cover of an average tipi needed twelve to fourteen tanned buffalo hides sewn together with sinew. This cover was tied to the last pole, which was put in the most westerly part of the cone. From there the cover was pulled around the poles to the doorway on the eastern side and tied from the bottom up. The woman then went inside the tipi and pushed the poles outward to make the cover tight. The bottom of

6 *putting up the tipi*

the tipi cover was tied down or held down with stones. All this took about half an hour. The tipi was made stronger during storms by tying a rope where the poles crossed each other at the top and staking the rope into the ground. In winter, a lining of hide five feet (one and a half meters) high was tied to the inside of the poles. Brush was stuffed between the lining and the cover to help the tipi stay warm. In summer, the bottom of the tipi was propped up to let in a breeze.

When a new tipi cover was needed, the woman of the family dried, scraped and cured some buffalo hides. Since a tipi cover is too big and heavy for one woman to make all by herself, the custom was to prepare a feast and invite other women to help. They would eat, smoke, talk and enjoy themselves as they put the skins together.

When the cover was finished, the tipi was set up with the door and smoke flap closed. A fire of sagebrush was lit inside to smoke the cover so that it would stay soft after rain. No help from the men was allowed. In some tribes, a woman had such authority over the tipi that all she had to do to divorce her husband was to throw his belongings out of the tipi.

Since there are hardly any trees on the prairies, long trips had to be made to the foothills of a mountain range or to the nearest valley to find long, straight lodge poles. The Indians traveled so much that poles wore down quickly and often had to be replaced every year.

Tipis were sewn by the women who also put them up and took them down.

A tribe could be recognized by the design and decoration of its tipis.

Painted tipis

Painted tipis were very special and were usually owned by chiefs and medicine men. The paintings on tipis could be a history but mostly they symbolized the visions a man received during a religious experience. Both men and women made pledges to some painted tipis in times of danger or when someone was sick. Painted tipis are still important today and are treated with great respect.

Some tipis were so big they needed eighteen buffalo hides sewn together. These large coverings were too heavy for one horse and had to be cut in half for travel and later rejoined. Tribes living in Canada often used brass buttons from the Hudson's Bay Company for this purpose.

Paints used for decorating the tipis were found in nature or traded from the white man. Reds came from ground rock, red earth, or the spring buds of pussy willows. Reddish brown was made by baking a yellowish clay over ash. Yellow came from near the Yellowstone River and could also be made from the gallstones of buffalo. Blue came from duck dung or a type of dark blue mud, and green came from a type of lake algae. These dry colors were mixed with hot water or glue made from boiled beaver tail or hide scrapings. Brushes were made from bone joints, chewed sticks or buffalo hair.

tipi liner

willow backrests

sweet grass altar

cooking fire

From the tipis of the Blackfoot of Montana, Alberta, and Saskatchewan we know the meaning of some designs. A dark ring at the bottom represented the earth, and a dark ring at the top, the sky. Round circles within these rings meant stars. Below the sky thin rings of color suggested a rainbow. In the space between the rings of earth and sky, animal figures were sometimes painted. These were special animals that had great spiritual power for the owners of the tipis. The most powerful animal was the buffalo. The most sacred were the mammals that live in the water – the beaver, otter, mink and weasel. The mythic thunderbird stood for lightning. Eagles and ravens were powerful helpers.

Tipi doorways faced east toward the rising sun. Inside, a small ring of stones formed the fireplace at the center. Behind the fire was an altar where sweet grass or other incense was burned. At the very back were the man's war trophies and ceremonial items. Beds, pillows stuffed with cotton wood floss and backrests made of willow strung with sinew lined the sides. Clothing tied in bundles and decorated cases, pouches and bags were tucked in the corner. Cooking utensils, food and riding gear were just inside the door. Where people sat and slept was important and depended on the customs of the tribe.

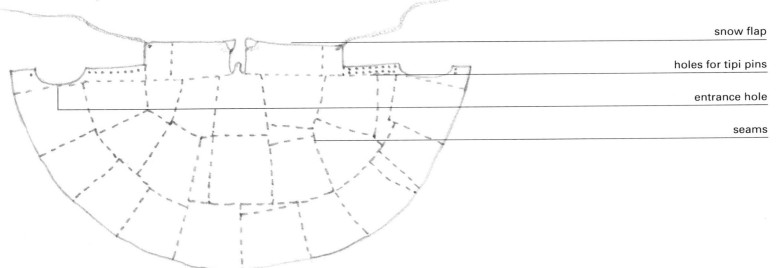

snow flap

holes for tipi pins

entrance hole

seams

tipi cover spread out on the ground

Some tipi doorways faced the rising sun. Inside, every object had a place:

ceremonial items at the back, beds and pillows along the sides.

The earthlodge

Earthlodge villages are different from anything we are familiar with today. First appearing in AD 700, they were built by tribes who farmed and traded for a living, as well as hunted. Like tipi dwellers, they moved to sheltered areas in the winter and built smaller versions of their summer lodges. They also used tipis, but only during buffalo hunting trips. Earthlodges were big and permanent. Since they could not be moved away from danger, villages were built on bluffs so that unfriendly visitors could be seen well in advance. The villages were surrounded with stockades and dry moats and often consisted of as many as 100 dwellings.

Just as tipis were arranged in a circle, villages were laid out in a way that had mythic significance. The Pawnee tribe believed that each village was started by a star. The supreme god of the Pawnee lived in the sky and his presence was represented by the shaft of light that came through the smoke hole. The Mandan built a shrine to their protector, the Lone Man, in a large open area in the middle of their villages.

A typical earthlodge was forty to sixty feet (twelve to eighteen meters) across and could be up to ninety feet (twenty-eight meters) wide. It housed a family and many relatives, about thirty to forty people. Food, especially maize (corn), was kept in deep pits dug into the floors. During the worst winter blizzards, people in the earthlodges could live on the food stored in the pits and were kept warm by the fire and the body heat of horses corralled inside.

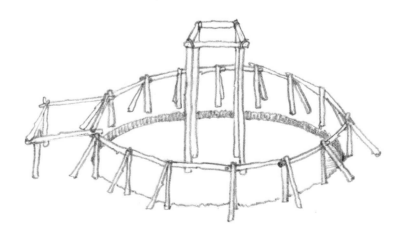

building the earthlodge

Between the lodges, storage pits and platforms were used for drying maize, meat and vegetables. The platforms were higher than a man's head to keep animals away from the food and had to be reached by a ladder. In fields outside the town, corn, beans, squash and tobacco grew. Each family had its own plot which was marked off by living fences of sunflowers. A warrior society policed the village.

To make an earthlodge, a circle the size of the lodge was marked off and dug out about a foot deep. This became the floor. Next, twelve thick posts about six feet (almost two meters) high were set in holes around the edge of the circle. These were connected with beams which rested in notches cut into the top of the posts. Side walls of small poles were leaned against the connecting beams. The next step was to put the four main posts in the middle. These posts, fifteen feet (four and a half meters) high, were set in a square ten feet (three meters) apart. More poles connected these at the top. To finish the frame of the lodge, many more poles were laid between the beams on the outside and those on the inside and tied together with fibers. Willow rods were then tied to the roof to cover the holes. On this, the Indians put prairie grass and a layer of sod and earth about a foot and a half thick. A large circular hole was left at the top for the smoke hole, and an opening for a doorway was left on the side.

screen of twigs over smoke hole

prairie grass

sod

hide partition

family stall

willow rods

Earthlodges, though large and permanent, were also arranged in a circle.

Children played on the rooftops while elders greeted the morning sun.

Inside the earthlodge

There were no windows in the earthlodges. Light came in only through the smoke hole at the top which was four feet (a little over a meter) wide. Entryways were about six feet (two meters) high and about twelve feet (four meters) long and usually faced east, like the doorways of tipis, toward the rising sun. To make the floors harder, the earth was stamped and flooded with water; then dry grass was piled on top and set on fire. The areas around the sides of the lodge were separated by hides or big sheets of willow matting hanging from the rafters on the ceiling.

Buffalo robes hung from the outer and inner doorways to keep out the wind. The fire pit, which was in the middle of the lodge, under the smoke hole, was about five feet (one and a half meters) across and dug a foot into the ground. The area around the fire pit, the hearth, was swept every day.

Tribes, like the Mandan, that weren't nomadic knew how to make pottery. Black pots and spoons made of horn hung near the fire and a mortar and pestle were placed in the ground.

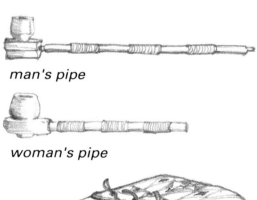

man's pipe

woman's pipe

Parfleche—hide case used for holding pemmican

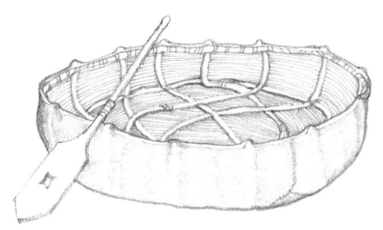

bull boat—the only water craft of the Plains Indians

An earthlodge was snug and comfortable. In some tribes, beds, with hide curtains around them, lined the walls. Storage pits were used like miniature cellars to keep corn, dried meat, skins and extra clothing. Saddlebags, rawhide pouches, shields and weapons hung from posts. An altar in the back was decorated with two buffalo skulls. There was a corral for the horses. In another corner there might be a sweatbath, or sauna, made with branches and covered with hide. The roof of the earthlodge was sometimes littered with buffalo skulls, boats made of skin, pottery and sleds. Children often played on it, and elders would go up there to greet the sunrise and sunset.

Women owned the earthlodges. They directed their building, and inherited them from their mothers. The Indians believed that a woman's ability to have strong, healthy children was connected with the fertility of the soil, and the earthlodge.

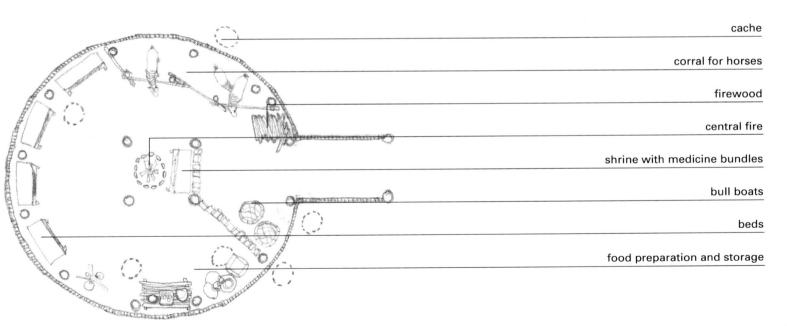

cache

corral for horses

firewood

central fire

shrine with medicine bundles

bull boats

beds

food preparation and storage

floor plan, the earthlodge of the Hadatsa

The earthlodge was spacious but the only light came from the smoke hole.

In winter, horses were corralled inside to help keep the interiors warm.

Other buildings of the Plains Indians

Many other structures besides the tipi and earthlodge were built on the Plains. These included arbors used for outdoor kitchens, platforms for food, storage pits, large structures in which the Sun Dance was held and sweatlodges.

Burial platforms were put up where "the dead live." Bodies were wrapped in buffalo robes and put on platforms built on stilts or tied in trees so that they would not be disturbed by wild animals. Cooking tipis were sometimes built during heat waves. To make one, Indians just cut off the bottom few feet of an old tipi cover to allow ventilation. Hunters out on a long chase sometimes dug a hole by a river for shelter during the night. During winter, a hole might be dug in a snowbank and the floor lined with buffalo chips for insulation.

The Sun Dance, the most important festival for many Plains Indian tribes, required a large and open structure forty to fifty feet (twelve to fifteen meters) in diameter. Its walls were covered with brush. In the middle stood a sacred cottonwood tree; this had been cut down and carried carefully amid ceremony and song so that it did not touch the ground. The tree symbolized the center of creation, and the trunk was the passageway from man on earth to the great spirit in the sky. From the top of the tree spread beams made from tree trunks. The crotch of the tree was stuffed with willow branches or buffalo grass to represent the nest of the thunderbird. Sometimes a buffalo head hung from the central pole. People ate

old women's society lodge

sweatlodge

and danced for days. Warriors wanting to prove themselves pierced their skin with wooden skewers attached to the pole by a leather strap as an offering to the great spirit. "Oh, Great Spirit of the Sun," a warrior might say, "I cannot offer you animals or plants for they are not mine to offer. They already belong to the Great Provider. I, therefore, can only rightfully give you of my own flesh and blood."

A sweatlodge was a small hut made of hides draped on a frame of willow branches. It was, and still is, an important part of Indian ritual. The Indian goes naked into the hut and pours cold water onto hot rocks, breathing in as much of the steam as he can stand. Bunches of sweet grass are burned, a sacred pipe is passed, and he prays for blessings. Sometimes a bag of earth is put inside a sweatlodge so the earth can be purified as well.

The circle which formed the base of the tipi, earthlodge and other buildings is a powerful shape. Black Elk, the famous Oglala Sioux/Lakota holyman, said, "You have noticed that everything an Indian does is in a circle and that is because the Power of the World works in circles and everything tries to be round. The life of man is a circle from childhood to childhood. Our tipis were round, like the nests of birds. But the white men have put us in these square boxes. It is a bad way to live for there can be no power in a square."

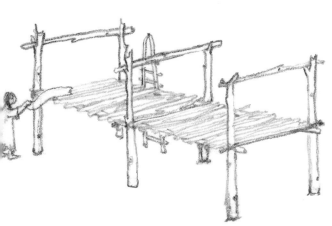

drying platform

tipi with cover rolled   *burial platform*

Large ceremonial structures – such as those used for the Sun Dance – as well as the tipi and painted tipi, are enjoying a revival. Even the earthlodge is being constructed for native festivals and museums.

24